Developing Reading Fluency

Grade 1

Written by
Trisha Callella

Editor: Teri L. Fisch
Illustrator: Jane Yamada
Cover Illustrator: Chris Ellithorpe
Designer: Mary Gagné
Cover Designer: Mary Gagné
Art Director: Tom Cochrane
Project Director: Carolea Williams

Table of Contents

Introduction

Learning to read is a systematic, learned process. Once children can read individual words, they need to learn to put those words together to form sentences. Then, children must learn to read those sentences fluently to comprehend not only the meaning of each word but also the meaning of an entire sentence. Children's reading fluency develops as they learn to break sentences into phrases and to "chunk" words together into phrases as they read. As children read sentences in phrases, they develop better comprehension of each sentence's meaning.

Use the lessons in *Developing Reading Fluency* to meet district, state, and national reading standards as you teach children how to develop reading fluency. The first five sections are arranged sequentially to help you implement fluency modeling, fluency practice by children, and then children's application of fluency strategies. Use the activities to help children build upon the skills they learned in the previous section. The final section of the book contains additional instruction to provide intervention for children having difficulties. The book features the following strategies to improve children's reading fluency:

- **Interactive Read-Alouds:** Use modeled and choral reading with the whole class or small groups to increase children's listening comprehension and to give them experience with rereading short rhymed phrases.
- **Cheers and Chants:** Model how to correctly read text, and teach children to echo your phrasing and fluency. These activities use guided practice and choral reading with the whole class or small groups.
- **Read-Arounds:** Help children learn high-frequency and content words and practice reading text in phrases as they work in small groups.
- **Plays for Two:** Use these simple scripts to have children practice with a partner repeated oral reading strategies as they develop phrasing and fluency.
- **Reader's Theater:** Have children work in groups of four to practice rereading a script until they can fluently read their part in front of an audience. Use the performances as a culminating activity to have children apply all the reading strategies they have learned.
- **Intervention Instruction:** Use these activities with individuals or small groups to intervene with children who still struggle with reading fluency. These activities enable children to identify and practice expression, intonation, and the natural flow of fluency.

The activities in this book provide children with a variety of reading experiences. The themes and genres included in each section will motivate children to not only read the text but to read with expression, intonation, and a natural flow. Children will build enthusiasm and confidence as they begin to increase their comprehension and as they successfully apply reading strategies to their everyday reading!

Reading fluency is the ability to read with expression, intonation, and a natural flow that sounds like talking. Fluency is not the speed at which one reads. That is the reading rate. A fluent reader does read quickly; however, he or she also focuses on phrased units of meaning. A child may read quickly but may not necessarily be fluent. Children who read too quickly often skip over punctuation. This inhibits comprehension because punctuation helps convey meaning. Fluent readers have developed automaticity. This means that they have a solid bank of sight words on which they can rely and that are automatic. Fluent readers can then focus their reading on understanding the message rather than decoding the text. Reading is decoding with comprehension. Fluent readers do both. They read without thinking about how they are reading, and they understand what they are reading.

What does a child who lacks fluency sound like?

A child who lacks fluency may sound choppy, robotic, or speedy.

How does repeated oral reading increase fluency?

Research shows that children increase their fluency when they read and reread the same passage aloud several times. The support that teachers give children during oral reading by modeling the text and providing guidance and feedback enhances their fluency development. Using this strategy, children gradually become better readers and their word recognition, speed, accuracy, and fluency all increase as a result. Their comprehension also improves because they are bridging the gap between reading for word recognition and reading for meaning.

Why should I worry about fluency when children are only emergent readers?

Bad habits can be hard to break. Research has found that poor reading habits stand in the way of children becoming fluent readers. Research has also found that children can and do become fluent even as emergent readers. Those emergent, fluent readers carry that fluency onto more difficult text and therefore have a higher level of comprehension. Fluency activities should be incorporated into every classroom, beginning in kindergarten with modeled reading, shared reading, guided reading, and independent reading.

How do fluency and phrasing work together?

Phrasing is the link between decoding the meaning of the text and reading the text fluently. Phrasing is the way that a reader groups the words. A lack of phrasing results in staccato reading, "word calling," and decoding. A fluent reader reads quickly in phrased chunks that are meaningful. Read the information on page 5 to learn more about phrasing.

Phrasing

A child who reads in phrases reads words in meaningful groups. Phrasing helps a child understand that the text carries meaning. A phrase is a group of words that the reader says together and reads together. The way the words are grouped affects the meaning. This is why phrasing affects reading comprehension.

What does phrasing sound like?

Consider how the same sentence can have different meanings depending on the way the words are grouped, or phrased. It clearly affects the comprehension of what is read. For example:

Patti Lee is my best friend.

Patti, Lee is my best friend.

Who is the best friend? It depends on how the sentence is read. In this example, punctuation also affects phrasing.

What causes incorrect phrasing?

A child may read with incorrect phrasing for a number of reasons. First of all, many children in first grade rely too much on phonics. This leads to a dependency on decoding. When children focus on decoding, they neglect the message. They turn into expert "word callers." Incorrect phrasing can also result from a lack of attention to punctuation. Some children ignore punctuation altogether, which will result in incorrect phrasing, will affect their fluency, and will hurt their comprehension.

What can I do to teach and improve phrasing?

1. Use the activities in this book. They are all researched, teacher-tested, and student-approved, and they will help children experience reading fluency success.

2. Stop pointing to each word during shared reading because that reinforces word-by-word reading. Once children can point and read with one-to-one correspondence, begin shared reading with a finger sweep under phrases. (Finger sweeps look like a stretched out "u.") This strategy models and reinforces phrasing.

3. Read and reread.

4. Model. Model. Model.

5. Echo read.

6. Make flash cards of common phrases to help children train their eyes to see words in groups rather than as individual words.

7. Tape-record children as they read. Let them listen to improvements they make in phrasing and intonation.

How to Use This Book

The activities in this book provide fun and easy strategies that will help children develop reading fluency. Getting started is simple.

- Use the Stages of Fluency Development chart on page 7 to assess children's ability. Take notes as children read aloud, and then refer to the chart to see at what stage of fluency development they are. Use this information to create a plan of action and to decide on which skills the whole class, groups of children, and individuals need to focus.

- Use the Fantastic Five Format on page 8 with the whole class, small groups, or individuals. This format provides a guideline for developing reading fluency that will work with any genre. Copy the reproducible, and use it as a "cheat sheet" when you give guided instruction. You will find the format effective in helping you with modeling, teaching, guiding, and transferring phrased and fluent reading to independent reading.

- Refer to the Teacher Tips on page 9 before you begin using the activities in this book. These tips include helpful information that will assist you as you teach all the children in your classroom to read fluently and, as a result, improve their comprehension of text.

Fluency Activities and Strategies

The first five sections of this book have been sequentially arranged for you to first model fluency, then have children practice fluency, and finally have them independently apply their newly learned skills. Each section has an introductory page to help you get started. It includes

- an explanation of how the activities in that section relate to fluency development
- the strategies children will use to complete the activities
- a materials list
- step-by-step directions for preparing and presenting the activities
- an idea for how to extend the activities

Each section opener is followed by a set of fun reproducible reading materials that are designed to excite and motivate children about developing reading fluency. Within each section, the readability of the reproducibles increases in difficulty to provide appropriate reading material for first graders who read at different levels.

Intervention Activities and Strategies

The last section of the book provides additional instruction and practice to help children who have difficulty with reading fluency. This section contains several activities designed for use with individuals or small groups. Each activity has its own page of directions that lists strategies, an objective, materials, and step-by-step directions. Reassess children often to determine their reading fluency level and their need for intervention.

Stages of Fluency Development

Stage	What You Observe	What to Teach for Fluency
1	• many miscues • too much emphasis on meaning • storytelling based on pictures • sounds fluent but not reading what is written down • playing "teacher" while reading	• print carries the meaning
2	• tries to match what he or she says with what is written on the page • one-to-one correspondence • finger pointing and "voice pointing" • staccato reading, robotic reading	• phrasing and fluency • focus on meaning • read like talking • high-frequency words • purpose of punctuation
3	• focuses on the meaning of print • may use bookmarks • focuses more on print than picture • no longer voice points • laughs, giggles, or comments while reading	• phrasing and fluency • focus on what makes sense and looks right • purpose of punctuation • proper expression and intonation
4	• reads books with more print than pictures • wants to talk about what he or she read • reads like talking with phrasing • reads punctuation with expression • laughs, giggles, or comments while reading	• shades of meaning • making connections

Fantastic Five Format

Step 1

Modeled Fluency

Model reading with fluency so that children understand the text and what they are supposed to learn.

Step 2

Echo Reading

Read one part. Have children repeat the same part.

Step 3

Choral Reading

Read together. This prepares children to take over the task of reading.

Step 4

Independent Fluency

Have children read to you.

Step 5

Reverse Echo Reading

Have children read to you, and then repeat their phrasing, expression, and fluency. Children have now taken over the task of reading.

1. Be aware of how you arrange rhymes, stories, and poems in a pocket chart. Often, teachers put each line in a separate pocket. When teachers do this, children do not recognize phrases and they begin to think that sentences always end on the right. (That is one reason why children often put a period at the end of every line in their writing journals.) Instead, cut the sentences or rhymes into meaningful phrased chunks so that children see and read what you model and teach.

2. If you use guided reading in your classroom, incorporate time for children to reread familiar books. Keep guided reading books that were once used for instructional purposes in bins that are color-coded to represent different ability levels. Have each child choose two books to reread as warm-ups every time you meet. This helps children put phrasing and fluency instruction into practice. Remember, use books that are appropriate to children's independent-reading level (books that can be read with 85 percent accuracy).

3. Write a daily Morning Message that follows a predictable format. Follow the Fantastic Five Format on page 8 to develop phrasing and fluency and improve reading comprehension.

4. Have a Friend of the Day tell you three things about himself or herself. Model for the class how to write the child's information in phrases on a piece of white construction paper. Read it in phrases and choral read it for fluency. Reread all of the information about previous Friends of the Day prior to writing about the new Friend. Bind the pages together into a class book, and have children read it independently or take it home to share with their family.

5. Once a child matches speech to print, do not allow him or her to point when reading. It is important to train children's eyes to look at words in groups rather than at one word at a time. While reading aloud, fluent readers look at many words ahead of what they read.

6. If children must use bookmarks to track words as they read, have them hold the bookmark just above the line of print they are reading rather than just under the line. When children use a bookmark under a line of print, the bookmark blocks the next line. This keeps children from reading fluently because they cannot see the ending punctuation. Try it—you will find that you cannot read fluently with a bookmark under the line you read. You will be amazed how this small change affects children's reading.

Learn to read with fluency!

Getting Started

Comprehension begins at the listening stage. Children understand what they hear before they understand what they read. That is why research supports reading aloud to children books and stories that are above their reading level. Reading aloud builds vocabulary, models thinking aloud, and models phrasing and fluency. This activity takes reading aloud a step further by including rhymed phrases that children will then use to apply the repeated oral reading strategy. The structure of this activity will keep children actively listening.

Strategies: repeated oral reading, modeled fluency, choral reading, active listening

Materials
• overhead projector/ transparencies or chart paper (optional)

Directions

1. Choose one story, and make one copy of the reproducible. (The story "The Spooky House" has two pages.) Copy a class set of the corresponding rhymed phrases. Or, as an option, make an overhead transparency of the reproducible or write the rhymed phrases on the board or chart paper.

2. NOTE: Do not photocopy the story for children. This activity is designed to build children's listening comprehension. They need to hear phrasing and fluency modeled by you in order to replicate it in their own reading.

3. Give each child a copy of the rhymed phrases, or display the phrases so all the children can see them. Read aloud the phrases, and have children practice reading them. (For the story "A Visit to the Vet," help children fill in the blanks with a sound and action word for each animal prior to reading.) Tell children that you will read aloud a story and that they will read aloud the rhymed phrases each time you point to them. (Point to the class each time you see an asterisk in the story.)

4. Read aloud the story. Model good phrasing, intonation, and fluency.

5. Throughout the story, stop at each asterisk, point to the children, and have them read the rhymed phrases, with increased fluency each time.

Extension

Many of the rhymed phrases lend themselves to movements. Make up silly movements that children can do as they read their part. This will maximize active listening. Try movements such as clicking tongues, clapping, stomping feet, moving hands like waves in the ocean, moving hands up together and then parting them in opposite ways, nodding heads, hopping, turning around, and cross-lateral movements.

A Visit to the Vet

Dr. Chapman is a veterinarian. He left his house early in the morning. He drove to the animal hospital. He had a full day ahead of him. He knew that he had many important patients who needed his help. He would perform two surgeries, help some animals feel better, and give three pets their shots.

As soon as he arrived, he started looking at the charts that told him about the pets he would see for the day. It is important for Dr. Chapman to know about the animals before they arrive. He was going to see some interesting animals!

His first patient arrived early. The patient was a golden retriever named Shiloh. ✳ Shiloh was at the vet to get his rabies shot. The shot keeps him healthy and protects him from getting rabies. Every dog ✳ gets a rabies shot, so Dr. Chapman has a great deal of practice. Shiloh ran into the room. His owners could barely control him. You could tell that he was one spoiled dog. ✳ After licking Dr. Chapman and almost knocking over the tissue box with his tail, Shiloh finally calmed down for his shot. He was rewarded with a bone. Wow! If only every patient arrived at Dr. Chapman's office this happy!

His second patient was his favorite type of animal. Since Dr. Chapman had special training with these animals, he knew exactly what to do. This animal, named Solo, was a pet horse. ✳ The horse was there for minor surgery. The surgery went well, and Solo was returned to her owner a few hours later.

Dr. Chapman's third patient was a common household pet. It was a male named Shadow. He was a black cat. ✳ Shadow had to visit the vet because he had a watery eye. His owners didn't know why it was watering. Dr. Chapman did! He gave Shadow's owners some eye drops to help Shadow feel better. Dr. Chapman said that Shadow's eye would be better very soon. A few days later, Shadow was a happy, healthy cat again! ✳

The next three patients were dogs. ✳ They were there for checkups. Dr. Chapman is always happy to see responsible pet owners bring in their pets for checkups. He likes to keep pets healthy as well as help them feel better when they are sick.

At the end of the day, Dr. Chapman went home to cuddle with his own pets—a bird ✳ and two Rottweilers. Dr. Chapman is a very happy vet.

A Visit to the Vet
Rhymed Phrases

_____, _____ is my sound.

I like to _____ all around.

_____, _____ is my sound.

I like to _____ all around.

_____, _____ is my sound.

I like to _____ all around.

_____, _____ is my sound.

I like to _____ all around.

Developing Reading Fluency • Gr. 1 © 2003 Creative Teaching Press

The Spooky House

Once upon a time, there was an old two-story house. It had to be at least 100 years old. Inside the house, there was a little old woman, a little old man, an old gray dog, a little black cat, and a family of little white mice.

One day, the neighbor next door went to knock on the door to deliver some mail that ended up in his mailbox by accident. As he walked up to the door, a little voice inside of him said, * He knocked on the door anyway. The door opened very slowly, creaking along the way. The man jumped back! He was surprised and a bit frightened. He didn't know what to do. He asked if anyone was home, but there was no answer. He didn't see any sign of the little old woman, the little old man, the dog, the cat, or the mice.

He knew that sometimes when people get older they can't hear very well, so he decided to yell into the house. There was no answer. He was worried for his neighbors' safety, so he decided to go into the house. Again, he heard that little voice inside of him saying, *

By now he was getting very frightened. Should he keep searching for the little old woman and the little old man, or should he listen to the little voice inside of him? He decided that any good neighbor would try to make sure that they were safe, so he walked into the living room. It was dark. He could see only a few things ahead of him. He was sure that the little old woman and the little old man were not there, so he walked toward the stairway. He looked up into the darkness of the second floor. Again he heard, *

He thought about leaving, but he just had to know that his neighbors were safe. He began walking up the stairs. He could hear the creaking of the stairs with each step that he took. The stairway led to a long hallway. He stopped and looked. Then he heard that little voice saying, *

He called out again for the little old woman and the little old man. There still was no answer and no sign of the dog or the cat. There were little white mice running around everywhere. That made his mind say a little bit louder, *

Again, he continued in his search for his neighbors. He was trying not to let the darkness of the house or the little white mice scare him. He told himself that it was just an ordinary house. The mice were probably his neighbors' pets. (Although, he did think that they had a few too many mice!) He opened the first door. He jumped back when he saw the cat run through his legs! Then he heard, *

The Spooky House

He continued on to the next door. When he opened it, he saw the dog sound asleep on a soft, cozy pillow. He didn't want to bother the dog, so he quickly closed the door. He moved on to the third and last door in the hallway. He heard some soft noises coming from behind the door. Should he open the door? No, he thought. He should knock first. He knocked. There was no answer. He still heard the sounds. Then, he heard his little voice saying, ✳

He just had to know what was going on! What was making the strange noises? Why didn't his neighbors answer him? What was behind that door? The voice in his head continued, ✳✳✳

As soon as he opened the door, he heard a loud

BOO!

He quickly ran across the hall, down the stairs, out the door, and back to his house! He was huffing and puffing so hard! He locked both of the locks on his door and peeked out the peephole. He should have listened to the little voice inside of his head. He knew it!

The next day, when he got home from work, he saw the little old woman and the little old man raking leaves in their front yard. He ran from his car to his house very fast! What were they doing? Where were they yesterday? Who scared him and why?

That night, he decided that it was silly for him to be so scared. The little old woman and the little old man had smiled at him when he got home. He made a decision. He would go outside, knock on their door, and ask them to explain what happened.

When he got to their door, he knocked very hard. There was no answer. His mind began to say, ✳ He knocked again. The door opened and the little old man said, "Hi. Do you want to play hide-and-seek with us?"

Developing Reading Fluency • Gr. 1 © 2003 Creative Teaching Press

The Spooky House
Rhymed Phrases

Do not go in there.
You don't know what's inside.
Do not go in there.
You should run and hide!

The Spooky House
Rhymed Phrases

Do not go in there.
You don't know what's inside.
Do not go in there.
You should run and hide!

Developing Reading Fluency • Gr. 1 © 2003 Creative Teaching Press

Best Friends

Themes: colors, friendship

Last summer, Trenton's best friend Chris moved away. Trenton missed him very much. Trenton's mom told him that he could visit Chris soon. Trenton worried that he may never see Chris again. Chris had moved to another state far away. They still wrote letters and called each other at least once every week.

In his last letter, Trenton told Chris about his new class. He talked about his teacher with the beautiful brown eyes. ✱ He talked about his new classmates. He even mentioned how much he liked where he sat in class. However, he did mention that school was just not the same without Chris. He said that he missed looking for worms in the wet, brown dirt with Chris. ✱ He said that he missed looking at the stars in the dark blue sky with Chris. ✱ Most of all, he just missed having a best friend.

One day, Trenton saw a "for sale" sign go up on the house next door. He was going to have new neighbors. He hoped he would meet a new friend, but his mom told him that he would not meet any new kids next door. Trenton told Chris that he was very sad.

The following week, when Trenton's mom got the mail, there was a bright green envelope. ✱ It was for Trenton. It was a letter from Chris. Trenton was so excited! He read it right away. Chris said that he missed Trenton very much. Chris's dad just lost his job, and they were moving again. Chris told Trenton that they would visit each other soon, and they would go to the pond to catch green frogs again. ✱ Trenton couldn't wait any longer.

Trenton went to find his mom. He asked her if he could fly on one of those new orange planes to visit Chris. ✱ She said that it wasn't possible right now. She had spoken to Chris's parents, and they were too busy packing, so Trenton couldn't visit their house on Lavender Lane. ✱ Trenton went to his room to write Chris a new letter.

Trenton waited three weeks for a letter back from Chris. It never came. Trenton began to wonder if they were still friends. He began to feel a little blue. ✱ His mother came in and told him that the new neighbors next door were downstairs and wanted to introduce themselves. She told Trenton to come down and say hello. Trenton said that he didn't feel like meeting anyone new. He just wanted his best friend back. His mother said that he would be feeling as bright as the yellow sun very soon. ✱

Trenton walked downstairs. He saw the new neighbors. His mom was right; he wasn't going to meet NEW friends. Guess who moved in?

Developing Reading Fluency • Gr. 1 © 2003 Creative Teaching Press

Best Friends
Rhymed Phrases

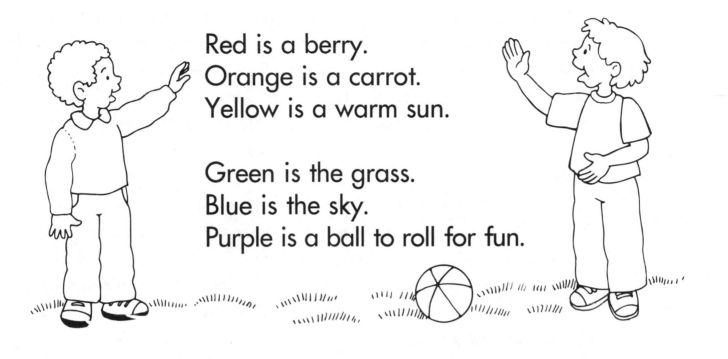

Red is a berry.
Orange is a carrot.
Yellow is a warm sun.

Green is the grass.
Blue is the sky.
Purple is a ball to roll for fun.

- -

Best Friends
Rhymed Phrases

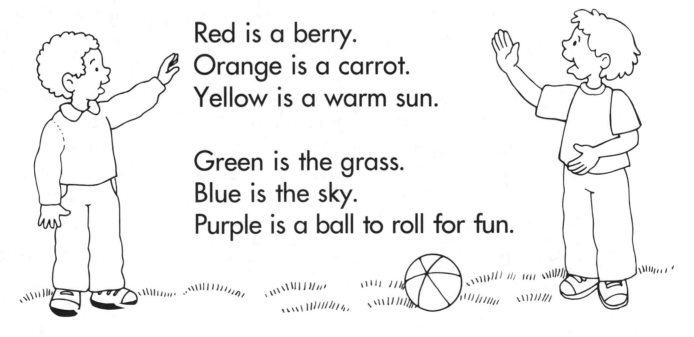

Red is a berry.
Orange is a carrot.
Yellow is a warm sun.

Green is the grass.
Blue is the sky.
Purple is a ball to roll for fun.

Developing Reading Fluency • Gr. 1 © 2003 Creative Teaching Press

Interactive Read-Alouds

Granny's Gorp

One rainy Saturday morning, Connor and his sister Leah woke up their mom. "Mom, can we go over to Granny's house today?" Mom said, "That is a terrific idea. I have some places I need to go anyway. I'll call Granny to see if it will work for her."

A few minutes later, their mom told them that Granny would love to have them over. Mom said, "Granny has a new special project for you to help her with. She would love to have you over at 12:00 today." "Great!" Connor and Leah shouted. Their mom said, "Go get ready and do your chores. We'll be leaving at 11:30."

Leah and Connor quickly finished their chores. Then, they played a few games together while they waited for their mother to take them to Granny's house. On the way, they talked about the crazy things Granny had planned for them before. The last time they were at her house, they all made mud pies with cherries on top! "I wonder what crazy thing Granny has planned for us today," said Connor. When they got there, Granny was ready with a hug for each of them.

"I'm so glad you wanted to come over today! I need some help making my Gorp," said Granny. Leah and Connor looked at each other. "Did you say, Gorp?" they asked. Granny said, "That's right! It's my secret mix. If you help me make it, you can eat it. There's just one more thing I need you to do. Every time we add a new ingredient, we have to say a lucky chant together to make sure the Gorp turns out yummy. Is it a deal?" "Sure," answered Leah and Connor, "but what is the chant?"

She told them, "It goes like this: Pour the _____ in. Mix it up with sticks. This is how we make Granny's Gorp mix!" Granny got a bowl, some sticks, and some different types of snacks.

Granny excitedly said, "Let's get started! First we need some pretzels. Are you ready for your part?" ✳ "Next, we need some nuts," Granny told them. ✳ "Okay, this looks pretty yummy, but now it's time to add a little sweetness to it. Let's pour in some chocolate candy pieces!" she said. ✳ "Now, let's see. Is it ready? We have salty pretzels, crunchy nuts, and sweet chocolate. What else do we have that we can add?" she asked Connor and Leah.

Teacher:
• Continue adding other food items (e.g., popcorn, cheese crackers).

Developing Reading Fluency • Gr. 1 © 2003 Creative Teaching Press

Granny's Gorp
Rhymed Phrases

Pour the _____ in.
Mix it up with sticks.
This is how we make
Granny's Gorp mix!

Granny's Gorp
Rhymed Phrases

Pour the _____ in.
Mix it up with sticks.
This is how we make
Granny's Gorp mix!

Cheers and Chants

An important part of learning to read is motivation and excitement. Through shared reading, you share that excitement with the class. You create a positive learning environment while reinforcing phrasing and fluency in reading, which are directly related to reading comprehension. Each Cheers and Chants rhyme is designed for the whole class or small groups.

Strategies: repeated oral reading, modeled reading, echo reading, choral reading

Materials
• chart paper, sentence strips/pocket chart, or overhead transparency/ projector

Directions

1. Choose a cheer or chant for the class to read. Decide how you want to present it to the class. (Each child needs to be able to see the text.) You can write it on chart paper, write it on sentence strips to place in a pocket chart, make a copy for each child, or make and display an overhead transparency.

2. Read aloud the cheer or chant several times. This will introduce children to the text and will model correct phrasing, intonation, and fluency.

3. Invite children to echo read or choral read the text. For "Living Things" on page 27, read aloud the chant to model fluency, then read it aloud using choral reading, and, finally, invite children to apply fluency by reading alternating lines.

4. To extend this activity, make copies of the reproducibles on construction paper or tagboard, and laminate them. Invite children to take home a cheer or chant to practice reading with their family.

Extension

Follow the Fantastic Five Format (see page 8) to incorporate modeled fluency, guided fluency, and independent fluency practice.

Step 1: **Modeled Fluency**—Display the chant or cheer. Read it as the class follows along.

Step 2: **Echo Reading**—Read one part. Have the class repeat the same part.

Step 3: **Choral Reading**—Read together. This prepares children to take over the task of reading.

Step 4: **Independent Fluency**—Have children read to you.

Step 5: **Reverse Echo Reading**—Have children read to you, and repeat after them.

Happy Birthday!

Theme: celebrations
(chant to the tune of "99 Bottles")

Happy, happy birthday!

This is your special day!

Happy, happy birthday!

We all want to say . . .

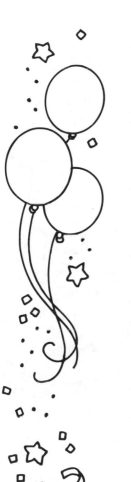

We hope your day is fun.

We hope your day is bright.

We hope that on this special day

You can blow out the candle's light!

Cheers and Chants

Patience

I try to wait my turn.

I try with all my might.

It is just a little hard

To wait my turn all day and night.

I am trying to raise my hand

Before I start to speak.

I'll try to get better

By the end of the week!

Developing Reading Fluency • Gr. 1 © 2003 Creative Teaching Press

Community

Theme: social studies

I live in a home.

My home is on a street.

My street is in a city

Too big to measure with my feet.

I live in a community

Where I live, shop, and go to school.

My community is full of people

Who help each other. It's so cool!

Cheers and Chants

Classroom Pledge

I will try

To do my best.

I will also try

To share my things.

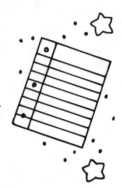

I will help my friends

And say nice words.

I will make the most

Of this day.

I am ready to learn!

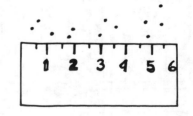

Developing Reading Fluency • Gr. 1 © 2003 Creative Teaching Press

First Grade Is the Best!

Theme: classroom motto

First grade is fantastic.

First grade is the best!

We get to read and write.

Forget that nap time rest!

We get to do some adding.

And graphs are so much fun!

I really like my teacher.

I am sad when the day is done.

First grade, first grade, first grade.

It simply is the best!

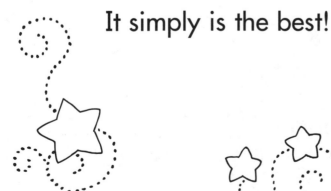

Developing Reading Fluency • Gr. 1 © 2003 Creative Teaching Press

Cheers and Chants

Sharing

You can use my crayons.

I can use your glue.

You can use my eraser.

I can use yours, too!

I will share with you.

You will share with me.

We know that when we share,

Good friends we can be!

26

Developing Reading Fluency • Gr. 1 © 2003 Creative Teaching Press

Living Things

Teacher   What do animals need to survive?

Children   Animals need food to survive.

Teacher   What else do animals need to survive?

Children   Animals need water to survive.

Teacher   What else do animals need to survive?

Children   Animals need shelter to survive.

Teacher   So, what do all living things need?

Children   They all need food, water, and shelter!

Teacher and Children Echo Response

Food (Food!), Water (Water!), Shelter (Shelter!)

Read-Arounds

According to research, one reason why children do not read with phrasing and fluency is that they do not have a solid base of high-frequency words and sight words, which is required for reading books independently. Research recommends activities that give children practice with frequently used words. This will in turn help with phrasing and fluency because children will not need to slow down to decode as often. The Read-Around cards in this section are already written in phrases (spaces between groups of words), so children can see and better understand how to read words in groups. The Read-Around cards are designed for groups of two to four children. This allows for optimal amounts of practice and active involvement. The phrases on the cards are short and simple to help children focus directly on reading phrases and practicing high-frequency and content words.

Strategies: phrased reading; repeated oral reading; active listening; reading high-frequency, content, and sight words

Materials

- construction paper or tagboard
- scissors
- envelopes

Directions

1. Choose a set of cards (e.g., color words, rhyming words), and copy the cards on construction paper or tagboard. (Each set of cards is two pages.) Cut apart the cards, and laminate them so that they can be reused throughout the school year. Put the cards in an envelope, and write the title (e.g., *Color Words*) on the envelope.

2. Give a set of cards to a small group of children so that each child has one to three cards. Review with children the pronunciation and meaning of the bold words on their clue cards so that they are familiar and comfortable with those key words (or preteach the words).

3. Explain that children will play a listening and reading game. Model how the game works and the correct answers with each group the first time children play using a new set of cards. Read aloud each child's cards, and then have children silently read their cards at least five times to build fluency. Discuss each question and corresponding answer so children can concentrate more on reading fluently than on determining the answer to the question as they play.

4. Tell the group that the child who has the clue card that says *I have the first card* will begin the game by reading aloud his or her card. After the first card is read aloud, have the child with the answer to the clue read aloud his or her card. Tell children to continue until they get back to the first card. (The game ends after a child reads *Who has the first card?* and a child answers *I have the first card*.)

5. Encourage children to play the game at least twice. Have them mix up the cards and pass the cards out again so that children read different cards each time.

Extension

Invite children to take home a set of cards. Have them teach their family how to play and practice reading the cards with family members. Encourage families to make additional cards.

Color Words

I have   the first card.

Who has the color   of the **sun**?

I have   the color **yellow**.

Who has the color   of the **sky**?

I have   the color **blue**.

Who has the color   of the **grass**?

I have   the color **green**.

Who has the color   of an **elephant**?

I have   the color **gray**.

Who has the color   of a **monkey**?

Read-Arounds

Color Words

I have the color **brown**.

Who has the color of a **carrot**?

I have the color **orange**.

Who has the color of a **cherry**?

I have the color **red**.

Who has the color of **snow**?

I have the color **white**.

Who has the color of a **road**?

I have the color **black**.

Who has the first card?

Developing Reading Fluency • Gr. 1 © 2003 Creative Teaching Press

Rhyming

I have   the first card.

Who has the word   that rhymes   with **thing**?

I have   the word **sing**.

Who has the word   that rhymes   with **sat**?

I have   the word **rat**.

Who has the word   that rhymes   with **sand**?

I have   the word **band**.

Who has the word   that rhymes   with **got**?

Developing Reading Fluency • Gr. 1 © 2003 Creative Teaching Press

Rhyming

I have   the word **hot**.

Who has the word   that rhymes   with **last**?

I have   the word **fast**.

Who has the word   that rhymes   with **funny**?

I have   the word **bunny**.

Who has the word   that rhymes   with **house**?

I have   the word **mouse**.

Who has   the first card?

Developing Reading Fluency • Gr. 1 © 2003 Creative Teaching Press

Animal Names and Movements

I have	the first card.
Who has	the animal with **stripes**?

I have	the **zebra**.
Who has	the animal that **barks**?

I have	the **dog**.
Who has	the animal that **chirps**?

I have	the **bird**.
Who has	the animal that **hops**?

I have	the **rabbit**.
Who has	the animal that **roars**?

Read-Arounds

Animal Names and Movements

I have   the **lion**.

Who has   the animal that **snaps**?

I have   the **crocodile**.

Who has   the animal with a **long neck**?

I have   the **giraffe**.

Who has   the animal with **fins**?

I have   the **fish**.

Who has   the animal that walks **slowly**?

I have   the **turtle**.

Who has   the first card?

Developing Reading Fluency • Gr. 1 © 2003 Creative Teaching Press

Synonyms

I have   the first card.
Who has the word   that means
the same as **nice**?

I have   the word **kind**.
Who has the word   that means
the same as **big**?

I have   the word **large**.
Who has the word   that means
the same as **small**?

I have   the word **little**.
Who has the word   that means
the same as **loud**?

Developing Reading Fluency • Gr. 1 © 2003 Creative Teaching Press

Synonyms

I have ___ the word **noisy**.
Who has the word ___ that means the same as **simple**?

I have ___ the word **easy**.
Who has the word ___ that means the same as **fast**?

I have ___ the word **quick**.
Who has the word ___ that means the same as **yell**?

I have ___ the word **shout**.
Who has ___ the first card?

Antonyms

I have   the first card.

Who has the word   that means

the opposite of **nice**?

I have   the word **mean**.

Who has the word   that means

the opposite of **big**?

I have   the word **little**.

Who has the word   that means

the opposite of **full**?

I have   the word **empty**.

Who has the word   that means

the opposite of **light**?

Developing Reading Fluency • Gr. 1 © 2003 Creative Teaching Press

Read-Arounds

Antonyms

I have the word **dark**.
Who has the word that means the opposite of **far**?

I have the word **close**.
Who has the word that means the opposite of **good**?

I have the word **bad**.
Who has the word that means the opposite of **dirty**?

I have the word **clean**.
Who has the first card?

Developing Reading Fluency • Gr. 1 © 2003 Creative Teaching Press

Counting by Fives

I have   the first card   to count by 5s.

Who has   the number   that comes after 5?

I have   the number 10.

Who has   the number   that comes after 10?

I have   the number 15.

Who has   the number   that comes after 15?

I have   the number 20.

Who has   the number   that comes after 20?

Developing Reading Fluency • Gr. 1 © 2003 Creative Teaching Press

Counting by Fives

I have   the number 25.

Who has   the number   that comes after 25?

I have   the number 30.

Who has   the number   that comes after 30?

I have   the number 35.

Who has   the number   that comes after 35?

I have   the number 40.

Who has   the first card?

Developing Reading Fluency • Gr. 1 © 2003 Creative Teaching Press

Plays for Two

Reading is a social event. People who enjoy books like to talk about them and recommend their favorite books. In classrooms, children are often asked to read alone. However, reading with a partner helps children develop phrasing and fluency through repeated oral reading while incorporating the social aspect of reading. Each Plays for Two story is designed for a pair of children to read together. Children will read their parts many times (repeated oral reading strategy) to improve their phrasing and fluency. Then, they will give a final reading for another pair, you, or the whole class. This activity helps reading take on a purpose.

Strategies: repeated oral reading, paired reading

Materials
• notebook/clear notebook sheet protectors

Directions
1. Make two single-sided copies of a paired reading script for each pair of children. (Each script is two pages long.) Do not copy the pages back-to-back. The print bleeds through and is visually distracting to children.
2. Divide the class into pairs. Give each pair a set of scripts.
3. Introduce the text to each pair through guided reading. Then, give partners time to practice reading together. (Have children practice reading and rereading many times to help them develop phrasing and fluency.)
4. To help children develop oral language and public speaking skills in front of a group, invite partners to "perform" their reading in front of the class or for a small group.
5. Train children to give each other specific compliments on their performance. Have them use the words and phrases *sounds like talking*, *phrasing*, and *fluent*.
6. Store each paired reading script in a clear notebook sheet protector (front to back). Store the sheet protectors in a notebook to make them easily accessible for future use.

Extension
Invite children to use the cutouts from the Cake Props reproducible on page 60, the cutouts from the Turnip Props reproducible on page 63, or their own cutouts to make their story more interactive. Have children color the cutouts and glue them to craft sticks to use as props.

The Little Red Box

Genre: mystery

Characters: Friend 1 and Friend 2

Friend 1   What is in your little red box?

Friend 2   It is a secret.

Friend 1   Can you just tell me?

Friend 2   You have to guess first. I will give you some clues.

Friend 1   I like games. Do I ask you questions to get the clues?

Friend 2   Yes! You must have played this game before.

Friend 1   Is it alive?

Friend 2   No. It is not alive.

Friend 1   Is it a toy?

Friend 2   Yes. It is a soft toy.

Developing Reading Fluency • Gr. 1 © 2003 Creative Teaching Press

The Little Red Box

Friend 1   Is it a toy I could throw to you?

Friend 2   No. It is not a toy you could throw to me.

Friend 1   Is it a toy I could sleep with?

Friend 2   Yes. It is a toy you could sleep with.

Friend 1   Let me see. It is a toy. It is soft. I could not throw it. I could sleep with it. Is it a stuffed animal?

Friend 2   Yes. What animal is it?

Friend 1   If it were real, would it be wild?

Friend 2   Yes. It would be a wild animal. You love this wild gray animal.

Friend 1   I think I know what it is.

Friend 2   What do you think it is?

Friend 1   I think it is an elephant.

Developing Reading Fluency • Gr. 1 © 2003 Creative Teaching Press

Plays for Two

The Noise

Genre: mystery

Characters: Friend 1 and Friend 2

Friend 1   I am so happy that you asked me to come over.

Friend 2   I am, too. Did you bring your sleeping bag?

Friend 1   I did. Are you ready to go to bed? We have to get up early in the morning.

Friend 2   Yes, we do if we want to get to the game on time.

Friend 1   Good night, _____.

Friend 2   Good night, _____.

Friend 1   Did you hear that noise?

Friend 2   I did. What do you think it is?

Developing Reading Fluency • Gr. 1 © 2003 Creative Teaching Press

The Noise

Friend 1	I don't know, but I am scared!
Friend 2	Did you just hear the noise again?
Friend 1	I did. What do you think it is?
Friend 2	I'm going to get my dad.
Friend 1	Good! I don't want us to be in here alone.
Friend 2	Wait! I think I see something.
Friend 1	What do you see?
Friend 2	I can see a shadow!
Friend 1	Where?
Friend 2	Over there on the wall! **BOOO!**

Plays for Two

The Little Pig

Genre: narrative story

Characters: Reader 1 and Reader 2

Reader 1   One day, we saw a little pig near our house.

Reader 2   I went over to meet the three pigs.

Reader 1   Hello. Who are you?

Reader 2   Hello. I am Pinky Pig. I live down the street. Who are you?

Reader 1   We are the Three Little Pigs. We all live in this house.

Reader 2   My dad told me about you. You made the Big Bad Wolf go away.

Reader 1   Yes, we did. But he is going to come back soon.

Reader 2   How do you know he will come back?

The Little Pig

Reader 1   He likes to try to blow our house down. He always comes back.

Reader 2   Are you going to hide from him?

Reader 1   No. But we will look for him.

Reader 2   Can I help you look?

Reader 1   We can all look out for him. Come on! We can look for him from right here.

Reader 2   We can hide behind this rock.

Reader 1   Look! I see the wolf!

Reader 2   RUN!

The Rabbit and the Dog

Genre: narrative story

Characters: Dog and Rabbit

Dog   Hi, Rabbit. How are you today?

Rabbit   Hi, Dog. I am happy today. How are you?

Dog   I am happy, too. Do you want to play with me?

Rabbit   I love playing with you. What do you want to play?

Dog   We can run in the grass. I can run faster than you!

Rabbit   No, you can not! I can run faster than you!

Developing Reading Fluency • Gr. 1 © 2003 Creative Teaching Press

The Rabbit and the Dog

Dog   It is time for a race!

Rabbit On your mark, get set, go!

Dog   We can both run fast!

Rabbit It is a TIE!

Dog   I am so glad that you are my friend.

Rabbit I like you, too!

Friends

Genre: poem

Characters: Friend 1 and Friend 2

Friend 1   I like to eat apples.

Friend 2   I like to eat pears.

Friend 1   I like to see monkeys.

Friend 2   I like to see bears.

Friend 1   I like to play with animals.

Friend 2   I like to play with blocks.

Friend 1   I like to pick up flowers.

Friend 2   I like to pick up rocks.

Friend 1   I like the color purple.

Friend 2   I like the color red.

Developing Reading Fluency • Gr. 1 © 2003 Creative Teaching Press

Friends

Friend 1	I like to read in the grass.
Friend 2	I like to read in bed.
Friend 1	I like to look at the birds.
Friend 2	I like to look at the bees.
Friend 1	I like to play on the swings.
Friend 2	I like to climb up the trees.
Friend 1	I am not just like you.
Friend 2	You are not just like me.
Friend 1	But we still get along . . .
Friend 2	PER - FECT - LY!

Developing Reading Fluency • Gr. 1 © 2003 Creative Teaching Press

The Baby Tiger

Genre: nonfiction news report

Characters: Reporter 1 and Reporter 2

Reporter 1 Hello all of you in TV land! Do we have big news for you from the zoo!

Reporter 2 What is the big news?

Reporter 1 A baby was born! It is big news!

Reporter 2 A baby was born at the zoo?

Reporter 1 It wasn't a human baby. A new baby tiger was born last night at the zoo.

Reporter 2 Is that really big news?

Reporter 1 Yes! It is a special tiger! There are not very many of these tigers.

Reporter 2 Why is this tiger special?

Reporter 1 It is a white tiger! It is so pretty!

Developing Reading Fluency • Gr. 1 © 2003 Creative Teaching Press

The Baby Tiger

Reporter 2 Can the people out in TV land see the white tiger?

Reporter 1 The people can see the white tiger in two days! They can even take pictures!

Reporter 2 Wow! I think we need to do a special report. Do you want to go with me?

Reporter 1 Yes, I do. I love tigers!

Reporter 2 So do I!

Reporter 1 Be sure to watch us next week when we bring in some pictures of the baby white tiger.

Reporter 2 We may see you at the zoo!

Reporter 1 For now, have a nice day!

Developing Reading Fluency • Gr. 1 © 2003 Creative Teaching Press

Big News at _____ School

Genre: nonfiction news report

Characters: Reporter 1 and Reporter 2

Reporter 1   Hello all of you in TV land! Do we have big news for you!

Reporter 2   We went over to _____ School and saw some great readers!

Reporter 1   All of the kids at _____ School can read books!

Reporter 2   Wow! That is great! Did you ask them what books they like to read?

Reporter 1   Yes, I did! They like to read so many kinds of books! I asked one boy to pick out the best book.

Reporter 2   What book did he give you?

Reporter 1   He came over with a huge pile of books! He said he could not pick just one.

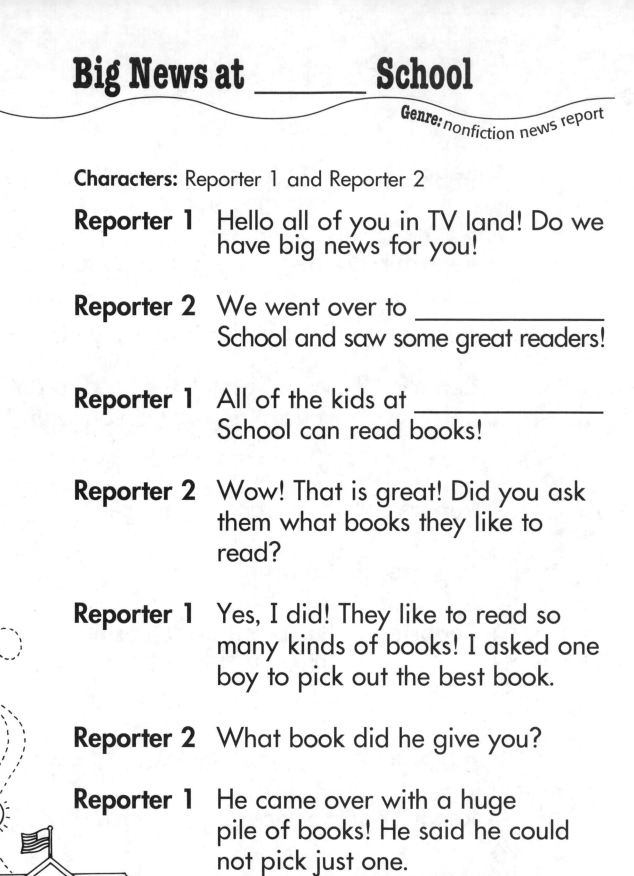

Developing Reading Fluency • Gr. 1 © 2003 Creative Teaching Press

Big News at _____ School

Reporter 2   Wow! He must really like to read!

Reporter 1   He said that he reads a book to his sister every night.

Reporter 2   That is so sweet. How old is his sister?

Reporter 1   She is just a little baby. He says he needs to read to her now so she will be a good reader like him.

Reporter 2   Wow! Did he read a book to you?

Reporter 1   Yes, he read a great book called The Big Pig.

Reporter 2   Did you like it?

Reporter 1   It was great! You need to go see the great readers at _____ School next time. It will make your day!

Developing Reading Fluency • Gr. 1 © 2003 Creative Teaching Press

Plays for Two

Ten Little Bunnies

Genre: *poem*

Characters: Friend 1 and Friend 2

Friend 1   Ten little bunnies playing on a vine.

Friend 2   One hopped away, so that left only nine.

Friend 1   Nine little bunnies trying to skate.

Friend 2   One fell down, so that left only eight.

Friend 1   Eight little bunnies counting to eleven.

Friend 2   One fell asleep, so that left only seven.

Friend 1   Seven little bunnies chewing on sticks.

Friend 2   One got full, so that left only six.

Friend 1   Six little bunnies watching a boy dive.

Friend 2   One ran away, so that left only five.

Friend 1   Five little bunnies hopping out the door.

Developing Reading Fluency • Gr. 1 © 2003 Creative Teaching Press

Ten Little Bunnies

Friend 2   One hopped away, so that left only four.

Friend 1   Four little bunnies hopping up on me.

Friend 2   One fell down, so that left only three.

Friend 1   Three little bunnies hopping up on you.

Friend 2   You picked one up, so that left only two.

Friend 1   Two little bunnies lying in the sun.

Friend 2   One hopped away, so that left only one.

Friend 1   Now there is only one little bunny resting by a tree.

Friend 2   He will not rest for long. Here comes a . . . BEE!

Developing Reading Fluency • Gr. 1 © 2003 Creative Teaching Press

The Cake

Genre: cumulative tale

Characters: Friend 1 and Friend 2

Friend 1   This is the cake that Kim baked.

Friend 2   This is the mouse that licked the cake

Friend 1   that Kim baked.

Friend 2   This is the cat

Friend 1   that chased the mouse

Friend 2   that licked the cake that Kim baked.

Friend 1   This is the dog that chased the cat

Friend 2   that chased the mouse

Friend 1   that licked the cake that Kim baked.

Developing Reading Fluency • Gr. 1 © 2003 Creative Teaching Press

The Cake

Friend 2   This is the mom who chased the dog

Friend 1   that chased the cat that chased the mouse

Friend 2   that licked the cake that Kim baked.

Friend 1   This is the dad.

Friend 2   Guess what he did!

Friend 1   While the mom chased the dog

Friend 2   that chased the cat that chased the mouse

Friend 1   that licked the cake that Kim baked,

Friend 2   the dad ate the cake!

Plays for Two

Cake Props

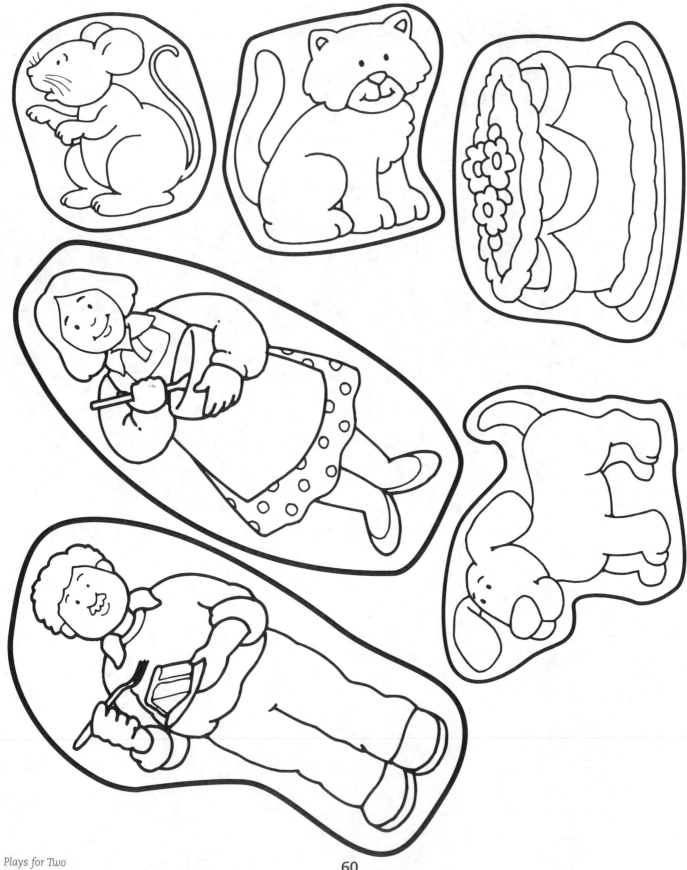

Developing Reading Fluency • Gr. 1 © 2003 Creative Teaching Press

The Enormous Turnip

Genre: cumulative tale

Characters: Friend 1 and Friend 2

Friend 1 This is the garden.

Friend 2 This is the turnip that grew in the garden.

Friend 1 This is the girl

Friend 2 who tried to pull out the turnip

Friend 1 that grew in the garden.

Friend 2 This is the boy

Friend 1 who pulled on the girl

Friend 2 who tried to pull out the turnip

Friend 1 that grew in the garden.

Plays for Two

The Enormous Turnip

Friend 2   This is the mom who pulled the boy

Friend 1   who pulled the girl who tried to pull out the turnip

Friend 2   that grew in the garden.

Friend 1   This is the dad who helped the mom

Friend 2   who pulled the boy who pulled the girl

Friend 1   who tried to pull out the turnip

Friend 2   that grew in the garden.

Friend 1   This is the dog that got the turnip out of the garden.

Friend 2   Do you know how the dog got the turnip out of the garden?

Friend 1   He dug a hole!

Developing Reading Fluency • Gr. 1 © 2003 Creative Teaching Press

Turnip Props

Reader's Theater

Reader's Theater is a motivating and exciting way for children to mature into fluent and expressive readers. Reader's Theater does not use any props, costumes, or materials other than the script, which allows the focus to stay on fluent and expressive reading. The "actors" must tell the story by using only their voices and must rely on their tone of voice, expression, phrasing, and fluency to express the story to the audience. Children are reading for a purpose, which highly motivates them because they take on the roles of characters and bring the characters to life through voice inflection. Each Reader's Theater script is designed for a group of four children. However, the scripts can be modified, if necessary. For example, children can double-up on roles to incorporate paired reading.

Strategies: repeated oral reading model for groups of four, choral reading, paired reading

Materials
- highlighters
- colored file folders
- sentence strips
- yarn

Directions
1. Make four copies of each play. (Each play is several pages long.) Staple together the pages along the left side of the script (not the top). Highlight a different character's part in each script.

2. Gather four folders of the same color for each play. Put one copy of the script in each folder. Write the title of the play and the name of the highlighted character (e.g., Recess Time, Mrs. Lee) on the front of each folder.

3. Divide the class into groups of four. Give each child in a group a folder of the same color (containing the same script).

4. Have children first read the entire script. (Research supports having children read all of the roles for the first day or two to fully comprehend the story.) Then, have children choose which part they will perform, or assign each child a part. Have children switch folders so that each child has the script with the highlighted character's part that he or she will play.

5. Write each character's name on a sentence strip to make name tags. Hole-punch the name tags, and tie yarn through the holes. Give each child a name tag to wear. Have children spend at least four to five days reading and rereading their part to practice phrasing and fluency.

6. Invite children to perform their play for the whole class, another group, a buddy class, or their parents.

Extension
Invite more advanced readers to choose a script and put on a puppet show with a group. (This type of performance is dramatic play, not Reader's Theater, because children use props with their voices to tell the story.) Invite the group to practice their lines, make puppets (out of paper bags, toilet paper rolls, or craft sticks), and perform the play.

Recess Time

Theme: conflict resolution

Characters: Mrs. Lee   Skylar
                  Jordan   Webster

Mrs. Lee

It's time for recess. You can line up at the door. Go outside and have fun!

Skylar

Do you want to play with me, Jordan?

Jordan

Yes. What game do you want to play?

Skylar

I think we should play in the sand.

Jordan

Good idea! I will help you make a big castle!

Webster

What are you doing in the sand?

Jordan and Skylar

We are making a big castle.

Webster

Can I play with you?

Jordan and Skylar

No. We want to make it all by ourselves.

Reader's Theater

Recess Time

Webster
I can help you make it bigger.

Jordan and Skylar
We don't want to play with you.

Webster
Well, then! I will step on your castle!

Jordan
I'm going to tell Mrs. Lee what you did! Mrs. Lee! Mrs. Lee!

Mrs. Lee
Hello Jordan and Skylar. What's the problem?

Skylar
Webster stepped on our castle! He is so mean!

Mrs. Lee
Webster, why did you step on their sand castle?

Webster
I wanted to play with them, but they said that I could not help them make the castle.

Mrs. Lee
So you stepped on their castle?

Developing Reading Fluency • Gr. 1 © 2003 Creative Teaching Press

Recess Time

 Webster
Well, they were being mean!

 Mrs. Lee
Did you step on the sand castle, Webster?

 Webster
Yes. They made me mad.

 Mrs. Lee
We have two problems.

 Jordan
I know what I did wrong.

 Skylar
I do, too.

 Webster
I know what I did wrong, too.

 Mrs. Lee
What are the two problems?

- Ask the audience what the two problems are.
- Invite the audience to suggest solutions to the problems.

Developing Reading Fluency • Gr. 1 © 2003 Creative Teaching Press

The Tree That Could Talk

Characters: Tree   Bird
                Squirrel   Caterpillar

Tree

I wish that I had a friend. I need a friend to talk to.

Bird

Who said that?

Tree

It was me. I am a tree. I want a friend.

Bird

I didn't know that a tree could talk!

Tree

It is a tree secret. We only talk when there is no one around.

Bird

Why do you wish you had a friend?

Tree

Well, I have to live my life in just this one place. I can't go out to make friends. I want a friend. I wish someone would come to see me.

Bird

I'll be your friend. I like to have friends. I like to talk, too. I will talk with you!

Developing Reading Fluency • Gr. 1 © 2003 Creative Teaching Press

The Tree That Could Talk

Tree

That would be nice. Will you make a nest on one of my branches and live here? I am strong. I will keep you safe.

Bird

I would love to build a nest here. You are so nice. Thank you!

Tree

What is that tickling my trunk?

Bird

That is my little friend the squirrel. He warns me when a cat is close by.

Tree

Can he be my friend, too?

Bird

I'll ask him. Squirrel, do you want to make a new friend?

Squirrel

Yes.

Bird

This tree is my new friend. He can talk just like us. He wants to be your friend, too.

Developing Reading Fluency • Gr. 1 © 2003 Creative Teaching Press

Reader's Theater

The Tree That Could Talk

Squirrel

I will be his friend. He helps me hide my nuts for the winter. I hide them in his roots and branches.

Bird

Great! We can all be friends.

Caterpillar

I was just lying on this branch up here. I think you need more friends. I want to be your friend, too.

Tree

Wow! We can all be friends!

Bird and Squirrel

That is a great idea!

Tree

I will be strong to hold a nest, to store nuts, and to let a caterpillar rest on me.

Bird

I will watch the sky for us. I will make a nest.

Squirrel

I will watch the ground for us.

Developing Reading Fluency • Gr. 1 © 2003 Creative Teaching Press

The Tree That Could Talk

Tree
Wow! We can all be friends! We can live and talk together.

Caterpillar
I have a secret. One day, I will turn into a butterfly. I will fly like the bird.

Tree and Squirrel
Wow!

Caterpillar
Can I still be your friend? I will land on your branches to talk to you.

Tree
You can always be my friend.

Caterpillar and Bird
Friends!

Tree and Squirrel
Friends!

All
Hooray!

Developing Reading Fluency • Gr. 1 © 2003 Creative Teaching Press

Reader's Theater

The Baseball Game

Theme: sports

Characters: Coach   Baseball Player 2
              Baseball Player 1   Baseball Player 3

Coach
The big game is today. Are you ready team?

Baseball Players 1, 2, and 3
We are ready!

Coach
Who is a great baseball team?

Baseball Players 1, 2, and 3
We are a great baseball team!

Coach
Who is going to be a good sport?

Baseball Players 1, 2, and 3
We are going to be good sports.

Coach
Who is going to try their best?

Baseball Players 1, 2, and 3
We are going to try our best!

Coach
It's time to play ball!

Developing Reading Fluency • Gr. 1 © 2003 Creative Teaching Press

The Baseball Game

 **Baseball Players 1, 2, and 3**
Go team!

 Coach
You need to try to hit the ball as hard as you can with the bat.

 **Baseball Players 1, 2, and 3**
Yes, Coach!

 Coach
When we are out in the field, you need to keep your eye on the ball.

 **Baseball Players 1, 2, and 3**
Yes, Coach!

 Coach
Who's first at bat?

 Baseball Player 1
I am, Coach. I am ready to hit a home run!

 Coach
That's what I like to hear!

 Baseball Player 1
I am out. I tried. I am sorry.

 Coach
You tried your best. You'll do it next time.

Developing Reading Fluency • Gr. 1 © 2003 Creative Teaching Press

Reader's Theater

The Baseball Game

Baseball Player 2
My turn. I will try my best, too.

Baseball Player 3
Good luck!

Baseball Player 2
I got out, too. I tried. I just couldn't hit that ball.

Coach
You did try. Who's next at bat?

Baseball Player 3
I am. I think I am ready. I will try my best.

Baseball Players 1 and 2
Good luck!

Baseball Player 3
I got out, too. Now we have three outs. I'm sorry!

Coach
You don't need to be sorry. You tried your best. That is all that I ask for!

Baseball Players 1, 2, and 3
Thanks, Coach! We'll keep trying to hit that ball!

Coach
Let's go get that other team out!

Developing Reading Fluency • Gr. 1 © 2003 Creative Teaching Press

Learning to Ride a Bike

Characters: Narrator   Keith
               Jill   Mom

Narrator

It is Keith's birthday. He is seven years old.

Keith

Thank you for the bike, Mom. I wish I could ride it.

Jill

You can do it. You just have to try. It took me a long time to learn how to ride a bike, too.

Mom

Do you want to try right now?

Jill

Yes, Keith. You will never learn how until you give it a try.

Keith

Okay, okay! I will try!

Narrator

Keith, Jill, and Mom went out into the front yard. Keith sat on his new bike.

Keith

I'm scared. What if I fall down?

Developing Reading Fluency • Gr. 1 © 2003 Creative Teaching Press

Reader's Theater

Learning to Ride a Bike

Mom

I will hold on to the back of the bike. I won't let go until you tell me to.

Keith

Do you promise not to let go?

Mom

I promise.

Jill

She did the same thing for me. That is how I learned how to ride my bike. You can do it, too!

Narrator

Keith began to pedal on his bike. Mom walked behind the bike to hold on to the seat.

Keith

I'm riding the bike! Wow! Okay, Mom, you can let go now.

Narrator

Mom lets go, and Keith falls down. He is crying. He is mad.

Keith

You said I wouldn't fall down! You made me get hurt!

Developing Reading Fluency • Gr. 1 © 2003 Creative Teaching Press

Learning to Ride a Bike

Mom

I said I would hold on until you told me not to. You told me to let go.

Keith

I am never riding a bike again. I can't do anything right. I give up!

Narrator

Keith sits on the ground and starts to cry even more.

Jill

That's how you learn. You'll be fine. You just have to try again.

Keith

I am never getting back up on that bike! Never!

Jill

If you never try again, then you will never learn how to ride a bike.

Keith

I don't care! I don't need to ride a bike at all!

Mom

Keith, I think you should try it just one more time. I will hold on. I will not let go.

Developing Reading Fluency • Gr. 1 © 2003 Creative Teaching Press

Reader's Theater

Learning to Ride a Bike

Keith

Do you promise to hold on?

Mom

I promise that I won't let go until you tell me to.

Jill

You can do it. Try it just one more time!

Keith

Fine! Just one more time.

Narrator

Keith gets back on his bike. Mom holds on to the back. He rides down the street and back.

Keith

I did it! I did it! I can ride a bike.

Jill

I knew you could do it!

Mom

I am so glad you did not give up!

Developing Reading Fluency • Gr. 1 © 2003 Creative Teaching Press

The Gingerbread Kids

Theme: fairy tales

Characters: Narrator   Gingerbread Kid 2
                Gingerbread Kid 1   Fox

Narrator
Once upon a time, a little old lady baked two little gingerbread kids. They came to life and ran away from her.

Gingerbread Kid 1
Hurry! We need to run into the woods so she can't find us. She will eat us up! Run!

Gingerbread Kid 2
I am running as fast as I can! Look! I see a little house. We can stay there and rest.

Narrator
The two little gingerbread kids went into the house. They saw a table with three bowls of food. They saw three chairs. One chair was broken.

Gingerbread Kid 1
I need to take a nap after all that running! I want to go look for a bed up those stairs.

Reader's Theater

The Gingerbread Kids

Gingerbread Kid 2
I like that idea. I need a nap, too.

Gingerbread Kid 1
Oh, no! There is a little girl in that little bed.

Gingerbread Kid 2
We need to run before she sees us. We need to get out of the woods!

Gingerbread Kid 1
Run!

Narrator
The two little gingerbread kids ran down the stairs and out the front door.

Gingerbread Kid 1
Wow! That little girl might have tried to eat us. We need to watch out!

Gingerbread Kid 2
We can slow down now. There's no one around here. We need to get across that river so we will be safe.

Developing Reading Fluency • Gr. 1 © 2003 Creative Teaching Press

The Gingerbread Kids

Fox

Hello, gingerbread kids. Don't be scared. I am a nice fox. I think you just said that you want to go across that river.

Gingerbread Kid 1

Yes, we do need to get across the river. You look nice. Do you know how we can get over there?

Fox

I would be happy to help you. You can sit on my back, and I will swim you across. You will be safe.

Gingerbread Kid 1

Well, I don't know if that is a good idea.

Fox

Do I look like I will hurt you?

Gingerbread Kid 2

No, you do look like a nice fox.

Fox

It's the only way you can get to the other side.

Developing Reading Fluency • Gr. 1 © 2003 Creative Teaching Press

The Gingerbread Kids

 **Gingerbread Kids 1 and 2**
Let's go!

 **Fox**
Get on my back.

 Gingerbread Kids 1 and 2
Thank you!

 Fox
Oh, no, thank you!

 Narrator (*to the group*)
How do you think the story ends?

Developing Reading Fluency • Gr. 1 © 2003 Creative Teaching Press

Helping People in Need

Characters: Narrator   Kendra
                       Garrett   Sandy

Narrator

The day has just ended at school. Sandy, Kendra, and Garrett are friends. They play after school.

Kendra

Did you hear what Mr. Rock said in school today?

Garrett

Yes. He said there are people who need food.

Sandy

He said there are people who need clothes.

Kendra

He also said that there are people who need safe homes. We can help.

Garrett

How can I help? I can't build a home. I am only in first grade!

Kendra

You are so silly! I know we can't build homes. I do have a plan for how we CAN help. Do you want to hear it?

Helping People in Need

Sandy and Garrett
What's your plan?

Kendra
We can help the people who need food. We can ask our friends to give us cans of food.

Sandy
Then we can give the cans of food to the people who need them.

Garrett
What can we do to help the people who need clothes?

Kendra
We can ask our friends to give us the clothes that do not fit them anymore.

Sandy
Then we can give the clothes to the people who need them.

Kendra
Do you like my plan?

Sandy and Garrett
It's a great plan. We can start right now!

Developing Reading Fluency • Gr. 1 © 2003 Creative Teaching Press

Helping People in Need

Kendra
We need to split up the jobs.

Sandy
I'll make a note to ask for cans of food.

Garrett
I'll make a note to ask for clothes.

Kendra
I'll talk to Mr. Rock. He can help us find the people who need the food and clothes.

Sandy, Garrett, and Kendra
Let's go!

Narrator
The next week, the three friends met again. They met to talk about what they should do next.

Kendra
How is our plan coming along?

Garrett
I have four bags of clothes. So many people wanted to help out with our plan!

Developing Reading Fluency • Gr. 1 © 2003 Creative Teaching Press

Helping People in Need

 Kendra
How many cans of food do we have so far?

 Sandy
I think we have 65 cans of food. Mr. Rock is keeping them for us.

 Kendra
Mr. Rock said that he knows who needs the food and clothes. He's very happy that we want to help them.

 Narrator
The three friends gave each other hugs.

 Sandy
I feel so happy that I could help.

 Garrett
What can we do next?

 Sandy
I think we should try to help animals.

 Kendra
Great idea! I think I have a plan!

Developing Reading Fluency • Gr. 1 © 2003 Creative Teaching Press

Intervention Instruction

Every section in this book can be used throughout the year to teach, guide, practice, and reinforce reading with phrasing and fluency, which will improve children's reading comprehension. The following activities provide additional practice and instruction for those children who need more help with the strategies that will help them improve their reading fluency. Assess children's stage of fluency development often by referring to the chart on page 7.

Use the following activities with "robotic readers" to help them be successful. The activities in this section will help children focus on the following strategies: phrased reading, automaticity with high-frequency words, recognition of what fluency sounds like at the listening level, and active listening.

Each activity includes an objective, a materials list, and step-by-step directions. The activities are most suited to individualized instruction or very small groups. The activities can be adapted for use with larger groups or a whole-class setting in some cases.

Strategies: explicit fluency instruction, concept attainment

Objective: Each child will understand what fluency sounds like.

Materials

- red and green paper
- craft sticks
- children's books (ones that you have read to the class before)

Directions

1. In advance, staple a red and green paper back to back on a craft stick (one for each child) to make a sign that can be flipped around.

2. Ask children which color they think will represent "doing a good job" and which will represent "needs some help."

3. Explain to them that red usually means "stop," so it will represent "needs some help" for this game. Green will represent "doing a good job." (You can also make the phoneme connection of /g/ = *green* and *good*.)

4. Tell children that you are going to read aloud a story. Explain that as you read, sometimes you will read as though you are talking. Tell them that good reading sounds like talking.

5. Tell children to show the green side of their sign when they hear your good reading (fluent). Tell them to show the red side when you read slowly, ignore punctuation, or read too fast.

6. Read aloud the book. (It needs to be familiar to children so that they listen to your fluency more than the story itself.)

7. As you read, change your pace, intonation, and expression.

8. Repeat this activity with a different book.

Strategy: explicit phrasing

Objective: Each child will understand what phrasing sounds like and looks like using his or her natural language.

Materials

- 1" x 11" (2.5 cm x 28 cm) white paper strips
- thin black marker
- scissors (fancy cuts help children see the phrase breaks better)

Directions

1. Ask each child to say a sentence about one thing he or she likes to do (e.g., I like to sing).
2. Use a black marker to write each child's sentence on a separate paper strip while the child watches. Say each word as you write it.
3. Show the child that you wrote down what he or she said.
4. Model how to read the sentence in phrases.
5. Give the strip to the child to practice reading several times.
6. Have the child read the sentence until he or she can read it well, with proper phrasing. Cut the sentence into phrases as the child reads the phrases and watches you cut them apart.
7. Place the phrases on a table and mix them up.
8. Tell the child to put the phrases back in order and read the sentence with proper phrasing.

Strategy: explicit phrasing

Objectives: Each child will understand what phrasing sounds like and looks like in text. Each child will transfer phrasing and fluency to ongoing text.

Materials
- A Day at the Movies 1 and 2 reproducibles (pages 91–92)
- The Trip to the Zoo 1 and 2 reproducibles (pages 93–94)
- familiar children's books

Directions

1. Copy a class set of the A Day at the Movies 1 and 2 reproducibles.

2. Divide the class into small groups. Write in each blank the name of a child in the group you are working with.

3. Give each child the A Day at the Movies 1 reproducible. Read the text following the Fantastic Five Format (described on page 8).

> **Step 1:** Model how to read each phrase.
>
> **Step 2:** Echo reading—Read one phrase at a time as children repeat.
>
> **Step 3:** Choral reading—Guide children as they read with phrasing.
>
> **Step 4:** Independent reading—Have children read the phrases without you.
>
> **Step 5:** Reverse echo reading—Have children read the phrases, and then repeat them.

4. Give each child the A Day at the Movies 2 reproducible. (It has the same phrases as reproducible 1, but it is written in an ongoing text format and has an additional paragraph of related text. This reproducible is the KEY! It is very important that you do not skip this reproducible because children will practice transferring their skills of reading phrases fluently to reading sentences in a paragraph fluently.)

5. Choral read the reproducible together. Then, invite the group to read it aloud to you.

6. Repeat the activity with The Trip to the Zoo reproducibles for further practice.

7. Invite children to practice their phrasing and fluency by reading a familiar book. Easy guided reading books are perfect.

A Day at the Movies 1

_____ and _____

went to the movies.

They were hungry.

They got

a few snacks.

They got

two hot dogs

and a tub of popcorn.

They got

two candy bars

and some water.

Then, they went in

to see the movie.

Intervention Instruction

A Day at the Movies 2

_____ and _____

went to the movies. They were hungry. They

got a few snacks. They got two hot

dogs and a tub of popcorn. They got two candy

bars and some water. Then, they went

in to see the movie.

The movie was good. It was very funny. After the

movie, they went home to rest. It

was a fun day for two good friends.

The Trip to the Zoo 1

_____ and _____

went to the zoo.

They both like

to look at animals.

It was fun

for the friends.

They saw

two big lions,

three tall giraffes,

four fat elephants,

five funny monkeys,

and six long snakes.

The friends had fun!

Developing Reading Fluency • Gr. 1 © 2003 Creative Teaching Press

Intervention Instruction

The Trip to the Zoo 2

_____ and _____ went to

the zoo. They both like to look at

animals. It was fun for the friends. They saw

two big lions, three tall giraffes, four

fat elephants, five funny monkeys, and

six long snakes. The friends had fun!

The two friends liked the monkeys the best. They

were so funny! Before the friends left, they

took pictures of the monkeys.

Developing Reading Fluency • Gr. 1 © 2003 Creative Teaching Press

Punctuation Practice

Strategy: explicit phrasing

Objectives: Each child will understand why punctuation is so important. Each child will read punctuation by showing expression

Materials

- Punctuation Practice reproducible (page 96)

Directions

1. Copy a class set of the Punctuation Practice reproducible.

2. Give each child a reproducible. Read it following the Fantastic Five Format (described on page 8) for each example on the top half of the page. Read one sentence at a time.

> **Step 1:** Model how to read the simple sentence.
>
> **Step 2:** Echo reading—Read the sentence, and have children repeat it.
>
> **Step 3:** Choral reading—Guide children as they read the sentence with expression.
>
> **Step 4:** Independent reading—Have children read the sentence without you, using expression.
>
> **Step 5:** Reverse echo reading—Have children read the sentence with expression, and then repeat the sentence using their expression.

3. After reading the sentences on the top half of the page, discuss with children how the ending punctuation tells you how to read each sentence.

4. Invite children to read the sentences on the bottom half of the page without you. If children struggle, repeat the Fantastic Five Format.

Punctuation Practice

I won the game.

I won the game!

I won the game?

She ate my cookie.

She ate my cookie!

She ate my cookie?

The car is stuck.

The car is stuck?

The car is stuck!

It's a bear?

It's a bear.

It's a bear!

Developing Reading Fluency • Gr. 1 © 2003 Creative Teaching Press